Helping Hands

At the Police Station

Ruth Thomson

WAYLAND

First published in 2006 by Wayland,
an imprint of Hachette Children's Books

Reprinted in 2007

Editor: Laura Milne
Managing Editor: Victoria Brooker
Senior Design Manager: Rosamund Saunders

Design: Proof Books
Commissioned photography: Chris Fairclough
Photograph bottom page 21: Courtesy of Dorset Police

British Library Cataloguing in Publication Data:

Thomson, Ruth
Helping hands at the police station
1. Police stations – Juvenile literature
2. Police – Juvenile literature
I. Title II. At the police station
363.2'2

ISBN-13: 978-0-7502-4856-3

Printed and bound in China

Wayland
338 Euston Road, London NW1 3BH

Acknowledgements
The author and publisher would like to thank the following
people for their help and participation in this book: Richard
Newton, Pete Holland, Tim Gallivan, Chris Bean, Adrian
Bowyer, Nick Brown, Louise Busfield, Christopher Elsdon,
Paul Mellor, Gary Miller, Natalie Shaw, Joanna Wharton at
Wimborne Police Station; Andy Flanagan, Mark Hughes,
Chris Maidment and Paul McKenna at Verwood Police
Station; Tim Gooding, Malcolm Wilcox and Andy Fields of
the Road Policing Unit; Jon Sweet and Gary Evans at
Ferndown Police Station; Georgina Marlow from Eastern
Divisional HQ; Phil Mimms, Headteacher, children and staff
at Ferndown First School; Anita, Emma and James Scrase;
Veronica Baker at PG Stores, Wimborne and Elisabeth
Webb at Wimborne Library.

Contents

Words printed in **bold** are explained in the glossary.

The team

We work at Wimborne police station in Dorset. Our job is to help keep the town safe. We help people in trouble and try to reduce **crime** and prevent **antisocial** behaviour.

We work in **shifts**, so there are always police officers at the station day and night to answer urgent calls.

We have two patrol cars for driving around town and to **emergencies**. ▼

At the police station

We each have different jobs
to do at the police station.

I am the sergeant in charge
of the station. I make sure
it runs smoothly. ▶

▼ I am a police constable.
I **investigate** crimes and try to
detect who did them. Later I
write up reports about them.

How to call the police in an emergency

* Dial 999.
* The operator will ask, 'Which service do you require?'
* Say, 'Police'.
* Give your name and phone number.
* Say what the problem is and answer the questions the operator asks.
* Do not put the phone down until the operator tells you.

▲ I work in the front office. I am not a police officer. I am a member of police staff. I help people who come to report something to the police.

▲ I am a **volunteer**. I keep watch on the town centre on **CCTV** screens. I report anything suspicious.

Police uniform

As soon as we come to work, we change into our **uniforms**. Our uniforms help people recognise us easily.

▲ I wear this uniform inside the police station.

▲ I put on my police jacket and helmet when I go out on foot patrol.

10

▲ We each have a **unique** shoulder number.

Sometimes I wear a protective vest. ▶

▲ Back view of vest

Police **crest**

Hard helmet for protecting my head from knocks

The name of our police force

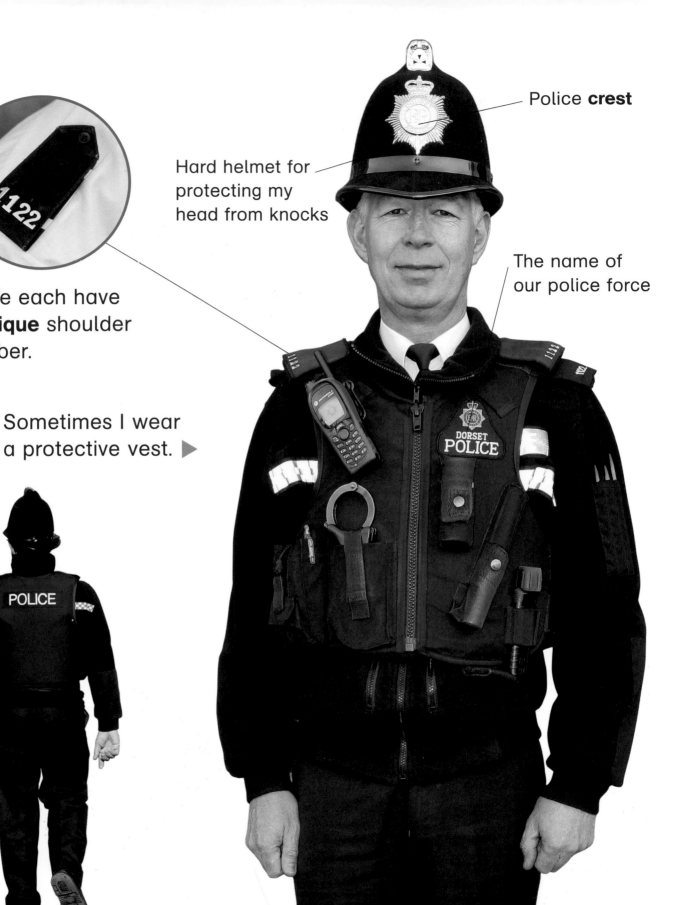

DORSET POLICE

Police equipment

We keep our **equipment** either
in our vest pockets or on a belt.

◀ Torch for night
time or searching
in dark places

Latex gloves to
wear when touching
something very
dirty or bloody ▶

▲ Pocket notebook and
pens for writing down
what we see, hear and do

12

handcuff key

▲ **Handcuffs** to put on a person who might hurt someone or run away

CS spray to stun someone for a short time. It is used to protect us and the public from someone violent.▼

◄ Asp which extends into a long baton▼

▼ **Warrant** card

Two-way radio, which can also be used as a mobile phone▼

The word 'police' in **Braille** for blind people

Community Police Officers

We are Community Police Officers. We **patrol** a particular area, known as a beat.
Our beat is the town centre.

We walk very slowly, watching out in case someone does something against the law. ▶

▼ Every morning, we drive around town. We check that no-one has broken into shops or offices during the night.

Sometimes, passing drivers ask us for directions or parking places. ▶

▼ People like seeing us. It makes them feel safe. They often stop to chat.

On the beat

I regularly visit shops and cafes on my beat. I have an advice desk at the local supermarket and school where people can come and talk to me once a month.

◀ I take photographs of graffiti so I can find out who wrote it.

I advise shopkeepers on how to protect their shops against **shoplifting**. ▶

If there is a problem and I need extra help, I call the police station on my radio. ▶

▼ More police officers speed to the scene by patrol car.

Under arrest

If we suspect a person of breaking the law, we **arrest** them.

▲ We take the **suspect** to the **custody centre** at the police station.

▲ The sergeant writes down the suspect's name, address, age and why he has been arrested.

The suspect takes off his shoes, belt, watch and money. We lock him in a **cell**. ▶

◀ I ask the suspect questions in an **interview** room. I record the interview on tape.

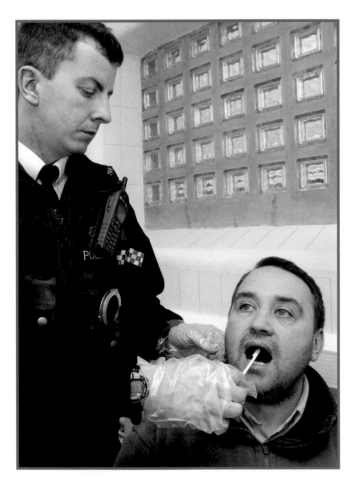

▲ I take a DNA mouth swab. This records the identity of the suspect, because everyone's DNA is **unique**.

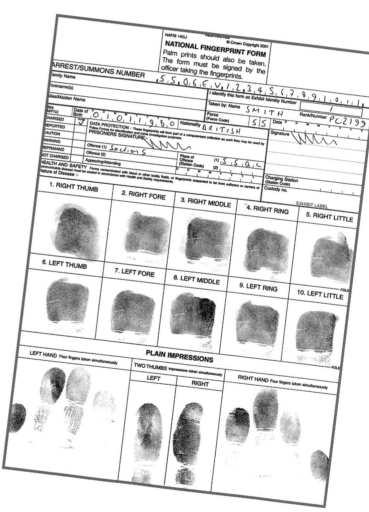

▲ We take the suspect's fingerprints. No two people in the world have the same fingerprints.

Community Support Officers

I am a Community Support Officer (CSO). My job is get to know as many people as possible in my area. People can ask me for support or advice.

torch

radio

I wear a **uniform**. The only equipment I carry is a radio and a torch. I can not arrest anyone. ▶

I go to schools
to talk to children
about road safety. ▶

▼ I helped young bikers mend
and repaint the local skate park.

Schools' officer

I am a schools' officer.
I visit local schools. I tell
children about the job we
do. I give talks and advice.

▲ I show children what we
wear and what we carry, so
that they can easily identify
a police officer.

◀ I discuss how
children might feel
if they are scared.

I discuss how children can keep themselves safe. ▶

How to stay safe

✳ If you are not met after school, tell your teacher.

✳ If you are lost, talk to a traffic warden, police officer, librarian or shopkeeper.

✳ Keep a list of useful phone numbers on you.

✳ Call 100 in a phone box to reverse the charges if you have no money or mobile to phone home.

✳ Dial 999 in an emergency.

✳ Never talk to a stranger or go with a stranger.

Road Policing Unit

We patrol roads in cars and on motorbikes. We make sure people are driving safely. We look out for stolen vehicles and vehicles used in crimes.

We hold a machine by the roadside to test if drivers are speeding. ▶

◀ Sometimes we ask someone to blow into a breathalyser. This tests whether they have been drinking alcohol.

▲ Our car is fitted with a video camera, so we can film the road ahead.

Cross the road safely

* Find a safe place to cross, then stop.
* Stand on the pavement near the kerb.
* Look all round for traffic and listen.
* If traffic is coming, let it pass.
* Look around again.
* When there is no traffic near, walk straight across the road.

If something, such as a fallen tree, is blocking the road, we drive down the middle of the road, slowing down the traffic safely. ▶

Road accidents

If there is a car crash or if someone is knocked over, we drive as fast as we can to the scene.

▲ We turn on the car's blue flashing light and headlamps as well as the **siren**. These warn other drivers to move out of our way.

▲ We put out road signs.

We set out traffic cones and flashing lights. ▶

▼ We wear bright yellow jackets and white caps, so people can see us easily. We wave traffic slowly past the accident scene.

Glossary

antisocial antisocial behaviour is harmful or unpleasant to other people

arrest to catch and take someone to a police station to be charged with a crime

braille a reading system for blind people using raised dots, which blind people read by touching them

CCTV (Closed Circuit Television) a fixed video camera that continuously films what happens in streets or shops

cell a room in a police station or prison where someone is locked up

crest the badge or symbol of an organisation such as the police

crime an action which breaks the law and for which someone is punished

custody centre a place with cells where suspects of crime are held

emergency a sudden dangerous event, such as a fight or an accident, which needs instant action

equipment all the things that people use for their job

interview a meeting when one person asks another some questions

investigate to find out about something

handcuffs two joined metal rings that lock over a person's wrists

latex thin stretchy rubber

patrol to walk or drive around an area

shift a period of time that a person works. Shifts are planned so that someone is working at all times

shoplifting stealing things from a shop

siren a loud horn

suspect someone who is thought to have done something wrong

uniform a special set of clothes that people wear for their job

unique the only one of its kind

volunteer someone who works somewhere without being paid

warrant a card that gives the police the right to arrest someone

Quiz

Look back through the book to do this quiz.

1 What phone number do you dial if you need the police urgently?

2 Name the equipment that police constables carry.

3 Why do police wear a uniform?

4 What is the area called that a police constable patrols?

5 How do road traffic police warn drivers of an accident?

6 What is the main job of a Community Support Officer?

Answers

1 999

2 An ID crest and warrant card, a two-way radio, a torch, a notebook and pen, CS spray, an asp and latex gloves.

3 So people can recognise them easily.

4 A beat

5 They put out road signs, traffic cones and flashing lights.

6 They get to know people in their area.

Useful contacts

Organisations that promote personal safety for children

Kidscape
2 Grosvenor Gardens, London SW1 0DH
www.kidscape.org.uk

The Suzy Lamplugh Trust
14 East Sheen Avenue, London SW14 8AS
www.suzylamplugh.org

Milly's Fund
Case House, 85-89 High Street,
Walton-on-Thames, Surrey KT12 1DZ
www.millysfund.org.uk

I never know what is going to happen each day.

29

Index

accident 26-27
arrest 18-19

beat 14-15, 16-17
breathalyser 24

CCTV (Closed Circuit
  Television) 9
cell 18
Community Police
  Officers 14-15
Community Support
  Officers 20-21
crime 6, 24

DNA swab 19

emergency 7, 9
equipment 12-13

fingerprints 19

graffiti 16

handcuffs 11, 13

interview 19

patrol car 7, 14, 17
police station 8-9

radio 13, 17, 20
Road Policing Unit
  24-25, 26-27

safety 15, 21, 23, 24,
  26
school 22, 23, 16, 21
Schools' Officers
  22-23
shoplifting 16
siren 26
speeding 24

uniform 10-11, 20

video camera 25
volunteer 9

30